ANCHORED

A Pocket Guide for Women Finding Strength, Hope, and Peace

Dr. Tamika Andrea

Anchored
A Pocket Guide for Women Finding Strength, Hope, and Peace

ISBN: 978-1-957904-21-4

This book is intended for inspirational and informational purposes only. It is not a substitute for professional counseling, medical advice, or mental health treatment. If you are experiencing a crisis or need immediate help, please seek assistance from a qualified professional or local support services.

Scripture quotations are taken from the Holy Bible, New International Version (NIV).

Printed in the United States of America.

First Edition.

DEDICATION

This book is dedicated to my cousin, Gena,
and to every woman carrying pain in silence.

For the women who smile while breaking inside.
For the ones fighting battles no one sees or asks about.
For those grieving, overwhelmed, exhausted, or quietly losing hope.

May these pages remind you that your life matters.
That your pain is seen.
That you are not weak for needing rest, support, or healing.

This book stands in the gap for every woman who needs to know she is not alone, and she never has been.

Table of Contents

INTRODUCTION
A Place to Breathe

This book was created for the woman who does not get to fall apart, even when her heart is breaking.

For the mother who still has to get up, pack lunches, answer questions, and show up for her family while carrying grief so heavy it takes her breath away.
For the woman who has buried dreams, relationships, seasons, or even a child, and still had to return to life as if the world did not just shift beneath her feet.

This is for the woman who loves deeply and gives relentlessly, even on her lowest days.
The woman who shows up as a mother, a wife, a sister, a friend, even when she is exhausted, overwhelmed, or quietly unraveling inside.

Some pain does not announce itself.
Some grief is swallowed so others don't have to choke on it.
And some strength looks like continuing to live when everything in you wants to stop.
You are not here by accident.

You picked up this book because something in you needed a place to rest, a place to breathe, a place where you didn't have to explain your strength or minimize your pain. A place that reminds you that even when life feels unsteady, you can remain anchored.

To be anchored does not mean the storm will not come.

It means the storm does not get to take you under.

This book is not about perfection.
It is about presence.
It is about giving you a steady place to land when your emotions feel heavy and your thoughts feel loud.

As you move through these pages, you will find words meant to encourage you, scriptures meant to ground you, reflections meant to steady you, and prayers meant to cover you. You will also notice intentional pauses — moments where you are invited to sit, breathe, and allow your own voice to be heard.
Because healing deepens when you give yourself permission to be honest.

This book is meant to walk with you not rush you.
Some days you may read one page.
Other days you may linger, reflect, or pray through a single paragraph.
Both are enough.

If you are carrying grief, this space is safe for your tears.
If you are rebuilding your strength, this space is safe for your process.
If you are learning how to love yourself again while still showing up for everyone else, this space is safe for your becoming.

You do not have to be strong here.
Take a breath.
You are in the right place.

CHAPTER 1

Anchored When Life Feels Unsteady

Finding Steadiness When Everything Feels Uncertain

The most life-shifting seasons of our life usually arrive without warning.

They slip in quietly through responsibility, loss, unanswered questions, or the slow accumulation of weight we never had time to put down.

You may still be showing up.

Still functioning.

Still doing what needs to be done.

And yet something inside you feels off balance.

Life can feel unsteady even when nothing looks wrong from the outside.

Even when you are doing all the "right" things.

Even when you are being strong.

Unsteadiness does not always mean chaos.

Sometimes it feels like standing still while everything around you quietly changes how you feel, how you move, and how sure you are of yourself.

It feels like holding it together without clarity.

Like carrying responsibility without certainty.

Like moving forward while quietly wondering when you will feel grounded again.

If this feels familiar, you are not failing.

You are responding to pressure.

There are moments when the weight is not dramatic enough to name, but heavy enough to feel.

Moments when you are strong for others, yet unsure who is holding you.

Moments when you are not falling apart, but you are not fully at peace either.

This is where being anchored matters most.

To be anchored does not mean you feel strong every day.

It means you choose not to let uncertainty define you.

It means you give yourself permission to pause, breathe, and steady your heart even when everything around you feels loud.

There will be moments when you do not have clarity.

Moments when you are making decisions while still healing.

Moments when you are moving forward, even though fear is trying to pull you backward.

And still, you remain anchored.

You are allowed to take things one step at a time.

You are allowed to rest without guilt.

You are allowed to ask for help.

You are allowed to admit that some days are harder than others.

Strength does not always look like pushing through.

Sometimes strength looks like staying grounded when life tries to shake you.

When you feel overwhelmed, remember this.

You do not have to have everything figured out to stay anchored.

You only need to stay connected to what keeps you steady. Your faith. Your values. Your purpose. And the truth that your life still has meaning.

Even here.

Even now.

You are not behind.

You are not weak.

You are not losing ground.

You are learning how to stand firm in the middle of change.

And that, in itself, is strength.

SCRIPTURES FOR THIS SEASON

God is our refuge and strength, a very present help in trouble. Psalm 46:1

When everything feels unstable, you are not asked to hold everything together. You are invited to run to the one who is present in trouble, not distant from it.

◊◊◊

Do not fear, for I am with you. Do not be dismayed, for I am your God. I will strengthen you and help you. Isaiah 41:10

This scripture does not promise that fear will never show up. It promises that fear does not get the final word because God remains with you.

◊◊◊

Come to Me, all you who are weary and burdened, and I will give you rest. Matthew 11:28

Rest is not weakness. Rest is wisdom. Coming to God when you are tired is an act of trust.

REFLECTION QUESTIONS

1. What feels unsteady in my life right now?
2. What am I trying to hold together by myself?

3. What helps steady my heart when my thoughts feel loud?
4. What is one small step I can take today instead of trying to solve everything at once?
5. Who can I reach out to for support without shame?

AFFIRMATIONS

- I am allowed to take things one step at a time.
- Feeling unsteady does not mean I am failing.
- God is present with me in this season.
- Rest is part of my strength.
- I can remain anchored even when I do not have all the answers.

DECLARATION

I remain anchored when life feels uncertain.

I release the pressure to have everything figured out.

I choose faith over fear, one moment at a time.

I give myself permission to pause and breathe.

I am held, I am guided, and I am not alone.

PRAYER

God, when my life feels unsteady, steady me.

Quiet what is loud inside of me, the thoughts, the worries, the pressure, and the fear that tries to take over.

Strengthen what feels weak, remind me that even in my moments of uncertainty, I am not without strength because You are with me.

Restore what feels shaken, rebuild the places in me that feel fragile, and help me stand firm even when life feels unpredictable.

Help me take the next right step without fear and without pressure, even when I do not have all the answers.

Teach me how to rest without guilt, and teach me how to trust You without needing to understand everything.

Remind me that I am held, that I am guided, and that I am never alone in what I am facing.

When I feel overwhelmed, anchor me in Your peace, when I feel uncertain, anchor me in Your truth, and when I feel weak, anchor me in Your strength.

Cover me with peace today, and allow that peace to quiet every anxious place within me.

In Jesus' name,

Amen.

CLOSING THOUGHT

You do not have to feel strong to remain steady.

Staying connected to God will anchor you, even when everything around you feels uncertain.

CHAPTER 2

Carrying Too Much for Too Long

Anchored in Strength

There is a kind of tiredness that sleep cannot fix.

It is the tiredness that comes from carrying too much for too long.

Carrying responsibility that has never been shared.

Carrying expectations.

Carrying the needs of others.

Carrying pain you never had space to process.

This kind of weight builds quietly. It does not always announce itself. It settles into your body, your thoughts, your spirit. You keep showing up, because you have to. Because people rely on you. Because stopping feels like failure.

But strength does not always look loud.

Sometimes strength looks like endurance.

Sometimes it looks like choosing to keep going even when you are exhausted.

And sometimes strength looks like admitting you are tired.

You may have learned to be strong early. Strong for your family. Strong for your children. Strong for people who depended on you when you did not have room to depend on anyone else. Over time, strength became survival.

But surviving is not the same as being supported.

Carrying too much for too long can make you forget that you are allowed to rest. That you are allowed to ask for help. That you are allowed to lay things down without guilt.

You are not weak for feeling tired.

You are human.

God never asked you to carry everything alone. The strength He gives is not meant to drain you. It is meant to sustain you. And sometimes, sustaining strength looks like learning when to stop.

You are allowed to release what is not yours to carry.

You are allowed to say no without explanation.

You are allowed to choose yourself again.

Strength is not measured by how much you can hold.

It is revealed by how wisely you know when to let go.

SCRIPTURES FOR THIS SEASON

He gives strength to the weary and increases the power of the weak. Isaiah 40:29

This scripture reminds you that strength is not reserved for those who already feel strong. It is given specifically to the weary. God meets you where you are, not where you pretend to be.

◊◊◊

Carry each other s burdens, and in this way you will fulfill the law of Christ. Galatians 6:2

You were never meant to carry everything alone. Strength includes allowing others to walk with you and share the weight.

◊◊◊

For my yoke is easy and my burden is light. Matthew 11:30

God does not add pressure to your life. He invites you to exchange what is heavy for what is lighter.

REFLECTION QUESTIONS

1. What am I carrying right now that feels heavy?
2. What responsibilities have I taken on that may not be mine to hold?
3. Where in my life do I feel the most exhausted?
4. What would rest look like for me in this season?
5. Who could I allow to support me without guilt?

AFFIRMATIONS

- I am allowed to rest without feeling guilty.
- Being tired does not mean I am weak.
- I do not have to carry everything alone.
- God strengthens me when I feel worn down.
- Letting go is part of my strength.

DECLARATION

I release what I was never meant to carry alone.

I choose rest without guilt.

I allow support into my life.

I honor my limits and listen to my body.

I am anchored in strength that sustains me.

PRAYER

God, I am tired.

I have been carrying more than I realized, and some of it I was never meant to carry on my own.

Help me recognize what is mine to hold and what I need to release, give me clarity where I have been confused, and wisdom where I have been overwhelmed.

Teach me how to rest without fear and how to receive support without shame, remind me that I do not have to do everything alone, and that asking for help is not weakness but wisdom.

Renew my strength where I feel worn down, restore the places in me that feel depleted, and breathe new life into every area where I feel exhausted.

Remind me that my worth is not tied to how much I carry, and that I am allowed to lay heavy things down without guilt.

Cover me with grace today, quiet the pressure I place on myself, and fill me with peace that settles my mind and steadies my heart.

Help me move forward with clarity, not confusion, with peace, not pressure, and with trust, not fear.

In Jesus' name,

Amen.

CLOSING THOUGHT

Strength is not proven by how much you carry.

It is revealed when you choose to lay heavy things down.

CHAPTER 3

When Strength Feels Distant

Anchored in Identity

There are moments when strength does not disappear, but it feels far away.

Moments when you know you are capable, yet feel disconnected from the version of yourself who once felt steady and confident.

This does not mean you have lost who you are.

It means you are tired.

When strength feels distant, identity can begin to feel uncertain. You may start questioning your worth, your purpose, and your ability to keep going. You may wonder why things that once felt manageable now feel heavy.

This season is not exposing weakness.

It is revealing exhaustion.

You are more than what you produce.

More than what you carry.

More than what others expect from you.

Your identity does not disappear when you feel worn down. It is not erased by grief, disappointment, or delay. It is not defined by how well you perform or how strong you appear.

Who you are remains intact, even on days when you do not feel like yourself.

There may be days when confidence feels quiet. Days when self-doubt creeps in. Days when comparison tries to convince you that you are falling behind. In those moments, it is important to return to the truth of who you are, not the noise of how you feel.

You are not your fatigue.

You are not your fear.

You are not your hardest day.

You are a woman of value. A woman of depth. A woman with purpose that does not disappear when strength feels distant.

Anchoring yourself in identity means remembering who you are, even when emotions are loud. It means choosing truth over comparison. It means releasing the pressure to prove yourself.

You do not have to earn worth.

You already have it.

SCRIPTURES FOR THIS SEASON

So, God created mankind in His own image. Genesis 1:27
Your identity was established before expectations were placed on you. You are created with intention, value, and dignity.

◊◊◊

Fear not, for I have redeemed you. I have called you by name; you are mine. Isaiah 43:1

This scripture reminds you that your identity is personal and secure. You are known, claimed, and held by God.

◊◊◊

I praise You because I am fearfully and wonderfully made. Psalm 139:14
Even when you do not feel strong, you remain wonderfully made. Your worth does not change based on your season.

REFLECTION QUESTIONS

1. When strength feels distant, what thoughts rise up in me?
2. What parts of my identity have I tied to performance or productivity?
3. How do I speak to myself when I am tired or discouraged?
4. What truths about who I am do I need to return to?

5. Where have I allowed comparison to steal my peace?

AFFIRMATIONS

- ❖ My worth is not tied to my performance.
- ❖ Feeling tired does not change who I am.
- ❖ I am valuable even when strength feels distant.
- ❖ I release comparison and self-judgment.
- ❖ I am anchored in who I am, not what I do.

DECLARATION

I choose truth over comparison.

I release the need to prove myself.

I honor who I am in every season.

I remember my worth even when strength feels quiet.

I am anchored in my identity.

PRAYER

God, when strength feels distant, remind me of who I am, remind me of who You created me to be, and help me to stand in that truth even when I do not feel it.

Quiet the voices that tell me I am not enough, silence every lie that tries to take root in my mind, and replace it with Your truth that I am chosen, I am called, and I am enough because You say I am.

Help me separate my worth from my performance, teach me that I do not have to earn love, approval, or value, and that who I am is not defined by what I do or how much I accomplish.

Restore my confidence gently, rebuild the parts of me that feel uncertain, and remind me that even in moments of doubt, I have not lost who I am.

Anchor me in truth when emotions feel overwhelming, steady my heart when my thoughts begin to drift, and bring me back to a place of peace, clarity, and confidence in You.

Remind me that I am still whole, even when I feel broken, and that I am still strong, even when I feel weak.

Thank You for knowing me fully and loving me completely, for seeing every part of me and choosing me anyway.

Help me walk forward today rooted in truth, not shaken by feelings, not defined by fear, but anchored in who You say I am.

In Jesus' name,

Amen.

CLOSING THOUGHT

You do not lose yourself when strength feels distant.

You are still who God called you to be, even in your trying seasons.

CHAPTER 4

Healing Takes Time

Anchored in Restoration

Healing is not a straight line.

It does not follow a schedule.

It does not move at the pace of expectations.

Healing unfolds slowly, often in ways you cannot see right away. There are days when you feel progress, and days when old feelings resurface without warning. This does not mean you are going backward. It means you are healing. You are learning to live within the limits God designed.

You are allowed to take your time.

So often, pressure surrounds healing. Pressure to be better. Pressure to move on. Pressure to stop feeling what you feel. But true restoration does not rush. It listens. It honors where you are. It allows space for what still needs care.

Healing does not erase your story.

It redeems it.

What you have walked through still matters. What you have survived still carries meaning. Healing does not require forgetting. It invites understanding, compassion, and grace.

There may be moments when you feel frustrated with yourself. Moments when you wonder why certain wounds still hurt. In those moments, remind yourself that healing is not about pretending the pain never existed. It is about learning how to live fully, even with scars.

Restoration happens when you stop fighting yourself.

When you allow what is tender to be tended to.

When you choose patience over pressure.

You are not behind in your healing.

You are not failing at restoration.

You are exactly where you need to be.

Anchoring yourself in restoration means trusting that God is working even when progress feels slow. It means believing that what feels unfinished is still being shaped carefully and with intention.

SCRIPTURES FOR THIS SEASON

He heals the brokenhearted and binds up their wounds. Psalm 147:3

God does not dismiss your wounds. He tends to them with gentleness. Healing is not forced. It is held.

◊◊◊

There is a time for everything, and a season for every activity under the heavens. Ecclesiastes 3:1
This scripture reminds you that healing has its own season. You are not late. You are not early. You are on time.

◊◊◊

But I will restore you to health and heal your wounds, declares the Lord. Jeremiah 30:17
Restoration is a promise, not a demand. God is committed to your wholeness, even when the process feels slow.

REFLECTION QUESTIONS

1. Where do I feel pressure to heal faster than I am ready for?
2. What parts of my story still feel tender?
3. How do I respond to myself when old wounds resurface?
4. What does patience look like in my healing journey right now?
5. Where can I offer myself more compassion?

AFFIRMATIONS

- I am allowed to heal at my own pace.
- Progress does not have to be perfect to be real.
- My story is not erased by healing.
- I choose patience over pressure.
- I am anchored in restoration.

DECLARATION

I release the pressure to rush my healing.

I trust the process of restoration in my life.

I honor my journey without comparison.

I allow grace to meet me where I am.

I am becoming whole, one step at a time.

PRAYER

God, teach me how to heal without rushing myself, help me to slow down and honor the process, and remind me that healing is not something I have to force.

Help me release expectations that do not honor my journey, the timelines I have created, the pressure I have placed on myself, and the belief that I should be further along than I am.

Teach me to give myself grace in the places where I feel behind, and remind me that I am still growing, still healing, and still becoming.

Tend to what is broken within me with patience and care, sit with me in the hard moments, and help me not to avoid what needs to be faced, but to walk through it with You.

Restore what has been wounded in Your time, not mine, and give me peace in the waiting, knowing that You are working even when I cannot see it.

Help me to trust the process, to embrace each step, and to believe that every moment of healing is leading me toward wholeness.

Thank You in advance for walking with me through every step of my healing journey, for never leaving me, and for holding me together even when I feel like I am falling apart.

In Jesus' name,

Amen.

CLOSING THOUGHT

Healing does not move on a timeline.

It unfolds with patience, grace, and care.

Every step you take still counts.

CHAPTER 5

When the Pain Still Lingers

Anchored in Hope

Some pain does not leave quickly.

Some wounds take longer to settle.

Some losses change you in ways that cannot be rushed or explained away.

Lingering pain can feel frustrating because it does not follow a timeline. You may expect it to fade with time, yet certain moments bring it back to the surface without warning. A memory. A date. A song. A quiet moment when everything slows down.

This does not mean you are failing to heal.

It means you cared deeply.

Pain that lingers is often pain that mattered. It represents love, attachment, dreams, and parts of your story that shaped who you are. Trying to force it away only creates more distance from yourself.

Hope in this season may feel quieter than before. It may not look like excitement or certainty. Sometimes hope simply looks like getting through the day. Like breathing through moments that feel heavy. Like choosing to stay present even when the ache remains.

Anchoring yourself in hope does not mean pretending the pain is gone.

It means believing that pain does not get the final word.

There may be days when you feel strong and days when grief feels close again. Both can exist at the same time. Healing and hope are not opposites. They often grow together.

You are allowed to hold space for what hurts without losing hope for what is ahead. Hope does not erase pain. It sits beside it and reminds you that life is still unfolding.

Even when answers are delayed.

Even when closure feels incomplete.

Even when the pain still lingers.

Hope remains.

SCRIPTURES FOR THIS SEASON

May the God of hope fill you with all joy and peace as you trust in Him. Romans 15:13
This scripture does not promise the absence of pain. It promises that peace and hope can exist even while you are still processing what hurts.

◊◊◊

The Lord is close to the brokenhearted and saves those who are crushed in spirit. Psalm 34:18

When pain lingers, God does not pull away. He draws nearer. You are not facing this season alone.

◊◊◊

For no one is cast off by the Lord forever. Though He brings grief, He will show compassion. Lamentations 3:31 and 32
This reminds you that grief is not the end of the story. Compassion still meets you in the middle of it.

REFLECTION QUESTIONS

1. What pain in my life still feels unresolved?
2. How do I usually respond when this pain resurfaces?
3. What does hope look like for me right now, even in small ways?
4. Where have I seen strength or growth in myself despite the pain?
5. What would it look like to allow hope to exist alongside my grief?

AFFIRMATIONS

- I am allowed to acknowledge pain that lingers.
- Hope can exist even when healing feels incomplete.

- My pain does not define my future.
- God is near to me in this season.
- I am anchored in hope, even on hard days.

DECLARATION

I allow hope to meet me where I am.

I do not rush my process or minimize my pain.

I trust that compassion surrounds me.

I believe that my story is still unfolding.

I remain anchored, even when the pain lingers.

PRAYER

God, You see the pain that still lingers in my heart, the places I have tried to move past but still feel, and the weight that has not fully lifted.

You know the parts of my story that still ache, the memories that still surface, and the wounds that have not completely healed.

Help me carry this season with gentleness, teach me not to be hard on myself in the process, and remind me that healing is not undone just because I still feel the pain.

Meet me with hope when the weight feels heavy, fill the spaces where discouragement tries to settle, and remind me that this is not where my story ends.

Remind me that I am not abandoned in this process, that You are with me in every moment, even in the ones that feel quiet, slow, or heavy.

Hold me close as I continue to heal, comfort me when emotions rise, and give me peace that steadies me even when I do not fully understand what I feel.

Help me to trust that I am still moving forward, even when it feels like I am standing still, and that every step I take is leading me toward wholeness.

Thank You for staying with me, for covering me, and for loving me through every stage of my healing.

In Jesus' name,

Amen.

CLOSING THOUGHT

Hope does not disappear because pain remains.

It stays with, even when healing takes time.

Sacred Spaces for Deep Loss and Care

These pages are different from the chapters before them.

They are not meant to teach or explain.

They are meant to hold you.

If you have reached this section, it is because something tender in you needed to be seen and protected. Take your time here. Read slowly. Pause often. There is no rush.

You are safe in this space.

For The Woman Affected by Domestic Violence

What you experienced or are experiencing is real.

It matters.

And it is not your fault.

Living through domestic violence can change how you move through the world. It can leave you questioning your safety, your judgment, and your worth. You may still feel on edge even when the danger has passed. You may struggle with trust, boundaries, or feeling fully at peace.

None of this makes you weak.

It means your body and heart learned how to protect you.

Healing after violence is not about pretending it did not happen. It is about reclaiming your sense of safety, one moment at a time. It is about learning that peace can exist again. It is about remembering that you deserve gentleness.

You are not broken because of what you survived.

You are here and that matters.

God sees every tear you cried in silence. He knows the fear you carried. He is near to you now, offering comfort, protection, and peace.

You are allowed to move slowly.

You are allowed to rebuild trust at your own pace.

You are allowed to choose safety again and again.

SCRIPTURE

The angel of the Lord encamps around those who fear Him, and He delivers them. Psalm 34:7

This is a reminder that protection surrounds you even when fear lingers. You are not alone.

PRAYER

God, You see where I am right now. You see what I am facing, what I am carrying, and what I am trying to hold together.

You know the fear that rises in me, the moments where I feel overwhelmed, and the times I do not know what to do next.

Be my protection in every moment. Cover me when I feel vulnerable. Give me wisdom to recognize what is safe and what is not, and guide my steps even when I cannot see the full path ahead.

Calm my mind when anxiety tries to take over. Steady my heart when I feel unsettled.

Remind me that I am not alone, even in the moments that feel isolating.

Give me strength for today. Not for everything at once, but for this moment, for this step, for this breath.

Help me not to lose myself in what I am going through. Remind me that I am still worthy, still valuable, and still deserving of love, safety, and peace.

When I feel stuck, show me that there is still a way forward. When I feel afraid, remind me that You are near. When I feel weak, be my strength.

Surround me with Your presence. Place the right people in my path. Open doors that lead me toward safety, toward healing, and toward peace.

And when the time comes for me to move, give me the courage to take that step.

In Jesus' name,

Amen.

If you are currently in danger or need immediate support, please know you are not alone.

The National Domestic Violence Hotline is available 24 hours a day at 1-800-799-7233 or you can text START to 88788.

You can also visit www.thehotline.org for confidential support and resources.

If you are in immediate danger, please call 911.

For The Mother Who Has Lost A Child

There are no words that fully hold this kind of loss.

And still, you are not alone in it.

The pain of losing a child reaches places language cannot touch, places only a mother's heart knows.

Your grief is sacred.

It is worthy of tenderness.

It deserves room to breathe.

Your love did not end.

Your motherhood did not disappear.

It continues in memory, in longing, in the quiet ways you still carry your child with you.

You may feel waves of anger, confusion, guilt, or deep sorrow.

Some days may feel unbearable.

Other days may feel quiet and heavy.

All of it belongs here.

All of it is welcome.

God does not rush your grief.

He sits with you in it.

He collects every tear and honors every memory.

You are not expected to be strong.

You are allowed to mourn fully.

You are allowed to miss your child openly, honestly, and without apology.

SCRIPTURE

The Lord is close to the brokenhearted and saves those who are crushed in spirit. Psalm 34:18

This promise does not minimize your loss. It assures you that God is near when your heart feels shattered.

PRAYER

God, hold me in my grief.

Carry me on the days I cannot stand on my own.

Comfort my heart with Your presence, especially in the quiet moments when the weight feels the heaviest.

Help me feel Your nearness when the pain feels overwhelming, and when the silence feels too loud to bear.

Remind me that I am not alone in this, even when it feels like no one truly understands.

Give me permission to grieve in my own way, at my own pace, without pressure and without expectation.

Hold the pieces of my heart that feel shattered, and gently remind me that love does not end, even here.

Stay close to me in every moment, in every memory, and in every breath I take.

In Jesus' name,

Amen.

For The Woman Who Feels Overwhelmed and Unsafe with Her Thoughts

If your thoughts feel heavy, loud, or frightening, pause here for a moment.

Breathe.

You are not alone.
You are not broken.
And you are not beyond help.

There are moments when emotional pain becomes overwhelming, when fear, sadness, or despair feel louder than your ability to cope.

Reaching this place does not mean you are weak.
It means you are human.
It means you are hurting.

You are worthy.
You are loved.
You are needed.

Your life matters.
Your presence matters.
Your future still holds meaning, even if you cannot see it clearly right now.

You deserve care, support, and protection in this season.
Asking for help is not failure.
It is courage.
It is choosing yourself.

You belong here.
The world is better with you in it.
Your life has value, even on the days it feels unbearable.

If you are feeling unsafe, please consider reaching out to someone you trust,
or seek immediate support.

You do not have to carry this alone.
You were never meant to.

If you are in the U.S. and need immediate support, you can call or text 988 to reach the Suicide & Crisis Lifeline (24/7).
If you are outside the U.S., please seek local emergency services or a trusted crisis line.

SCRIPTURE

For I am the Lord your God who takes hold of your right hand and says to you, Do not fear; I will help you.
Isaiah 41:13

This is a promise of presence and support. You are being held, even when your thoughts feel overwhelming.

PRAYER

God, quiet my thoughts when they feel too heavy.

Surround me with safety, care, and support.

Help me reach out for help when I need it.

Anchor me in this moment and remind me that I am not alone.

Remind me that my life has value and purpose.

In Jesus' name,

Amen.

A Letter You Never Have To Send

This is a safe space.

No one else will read these words unless you choose to share them.

This letter is not about fixing anything.

It is not about forcing forgiveness.

It is not about understanding what happened.

It is about release.

There are things you have carried quietly. Words you have swallowed. Feelings you have tucked away so you could keep going. Moments you replayed in your mind without ever having the chance to say what you needed to say.

Here, you are allowed to let them out.

You can write to the person or situation that hurt you.

You can write to the version of yourself that survived something painful.

You can write to God.

You can write to the situation that changed your life.

Say what you never got to say.

Name what hurt.

Acknowledge what you lost.

Express what you wish had been different.

You do not owe forgiveness in this moment.

You do not owe clarity.

You do not owe closure.

You owe yourself honesty.

This letter is not meant to reopen wounds.

It is meant to create space.

Space for truth.

Space for breath.

Space for peace to enter gently.

When you finish writing, you may keep this letter.

You may tear it up.

You may place it somewhere safe.

You may pray over it and let it go.

There is no right or wrong way to do this.

Releasing what has been held inside does not erase the past.

It loosens its grip on you.

You are allowed to move forward without carrying every word you never spoke.

You do not have to send this letter.

You do not have to resolve everything today.

For now, it is enough that you told the truth.

Let this be enough for the moment.

You are still safe here.

CHAPTER 6

Learning to Trust Again

Anchored in Trust

Trust does not return all at once.

It rebuilds slowly, carefully, often after being deeply shaken.

When trust has been broken, whether by people, circumstances, or experiences you did not choose, it can feel risky to open your heart again. You may find yourself guarded, cautious, or hesitant to believe that things can be different.

This is not weakness.

It is wisdom born from experience.

Learning to trust again does not mean pretending nothing happened. It does not require you to forget the past or dismiss the pain you endured. Trust after hurt looks different. It grows with discernment, boundaries, and patience.

You are allowed to protect your heart.

You are allowed to move slowly.

You are allowed to choose peace over pressure.

If trust feels complicated now, that makes sense.

When trust has been broken by someone close, by someone you loved, by someone you believed in, it can change how you move through the world.

Sometimes the deepest wounds do not come from strangers,
but from friends, family, or people who were supposed to protect your heart.

Trusting again often begins quietly, internally.
Learning to trust your own voice.
Your instincts.
Your ability to recognize what feels safe and what does not.

As you reconnect with yourself, trust can gently extend outward again,
in healthy, measured ways.

You do not have to trust everyone.
You do not have to trust everything.
You do not have to rush forgiveness or closeness.

You are allowed to be discerning.

You only need to trust what has shown itself to be steady, respectful, and consistent.

Anchoring yourself in trust does not mean pretending the past didn't hurt.

It means believing that not every experience will repeat what broke you.

It means allowing hope to grow without forcing it.
It means honoring your healing by choosing wisely.

Trust rebuilt with care is stronger than trust given without thought.

SCRIPTURES FOR THIS SEASON

Trust in the Lord with all your heart and lean not on your own understanding. Proverbs 3:5
This scripture does not ask you to ignore your experiences or your discernment. It invites you to place your trust in God even when your understanding feels incomplete.

◊◊◊

When I am afraid, I put my trust in You. Psalm 56:3
This keeps God as your safe place, not the people who hurt you. Fear and trust can exist at the same time. Choosing trust does not mean fear disappears. It means fear does not control your decisions.

◊◊◊

Blessed is the one who trusts in the Lord, whose confidence is in Him. Jeremiah 17:7
Trust rooted in God provides stability when human trust feels fragile.

REFLECTION QUESTIONS

1. What experiences have made trusting difficult for me?
2. Where do I feel guarded or hesitant to open up again?
3. How can I rebuild trust with myself first?
4. What boundaries help me feel safe?
5. What would trusting slowly look like in this season?

AFFIRMATIONS

- ❖ I am allowed to rebuild trust at my own pace.
- ❖ Protecting my heart is wisdom, not fear.
- ❖ I trust myself to recognize what feels safe.
- ❖ God guides me as I learn to trust again.
- ❖ I am anchored in trust that grows with time.

DECLARATION

I release the pressure to rush trust.

I honor my healing journey.

I choose discernment over fear.

I allow trust to grow gently and safely.

I am anchored in trust.

PRAYER

God, help me trust again without rushing myself.

Heal the places where trust was broken, and restore what feels guarded within me.

Guide me with wisdom and discernment as I move forward.

Teach me how to trust You even when I feel hesitant, and when fear tries to hold me back.

Help me recognize what is safe and good for me, and give me peace in the choices I make.

I place my heart in Your care, trusting that you will lead me gently.

In Jesus' name,

Amen.

CLOSING THOUGHT

Trust rebuilt with patience becomes a place of peace.

You do not have to rush what God is restoring.

CHAPTER 7

Anchored and Becoming

Moving Forward with Peace, Courage, and Faith

Becoming does not mean you have arrived.

It means you are still growing.

After everything you have walked through, the uncertainty, the weight, the healing, the lingering pain, the rebuilding, you are still here. Still breathing. Still learning. Still becoming.

Becoming is not about perfection.

It is about movement.

It is about choosing to keep going even when the path is unfamiliar.

You are not becoming someone new.

You are becoming more fully yourself.

There is strength in acknowledging how far you have come. Strength in recognizing the growth that happened quietly. Strength in honoring the woman you are now, shaped by experience, faith, and resilience.

You may not have all the answers yet.

You may still feel cautious.

You may still be healing parts of your heart.

And still, you are becoming.

Being anchored does not mean you will never feel fear again. It means fear does not control you. It means you know where to return when life feels overwhelming. It means you carry steadiness within you now.

You are allowed to move forward gently.

You are allowed to dream again without pressure.

You are allowed to trust that what is ahead holds meaning.

Becoming happens in small steps. In quiet decisions. In moments when you choose peace over chaos, truth over fear, and faith over doubt.

This is not the end of your story.

It is the beginning of a new chapter written with intention.

You are anchored.

And you are becoming.

SCRIPTURES FOR THIS SEASON

He who began a good work in you will carry it on to completion until the day of Christ Jesus. Philippians 1:6

This scripture reminds you that what God started in you is not abandoned. Your growth is ongoing and purposeful.

◊◊◊

See, I am doing a new thing. Now it springs up; do you not perceive it? Isaiah 43:19
Becoming often begins quietly. God works in ways you may not recognize right away, but new life is forming.

◊◊◊

If anyone is in Christ, the new creation has come. The old has gone, the new is here. 2 Corinthians 5:17
This is not about erasing your past. It is about allowing transformation to continue.

REFLECTION QUESTIONS

1. How have I grown through what I have walked through?
2. What parts of myself am I learning to honor more?
3. Where do I feel called to move forward with courage?
4. What does becoming look like for me right now?
5. How can I continue anchoring myself in peace?

AFFIRMATIONS

- I honor who I am becoming.
- I move forward with peace and intention.
- I trust the process of growth in my life.
- My past does not limit my future.
- I am anchored and becoming.

DECLARATION

I embrace the woman I am becoming.

I release fear of what is ahead.

I choose peace, courage, and faith.

I trust that my story is still unfolding.

I remain anchored as I grow.

PRAYER

God, thank You for walking with me through every season.

Thank You for the growth that has taken place within me.

Guide my steps as I move forward with clarity and peace.

Help me remain anchored as I continue becoming.

Strengthen my faith for what lies ahead, and quiet any fear that tries to follow me forward.

I trust You with what is ahead.

In Jesus' name,

Amen.

CLOSING THOUGHT

Becoming is not about arriving.

It is about trusting who you are becoming, even while you are still growing.

For The Mother Who Worries About Her Children

Worry has a way of finding mothers in quiet moments.

Late nights. Long days. Unanswered calls. Uncertain futures.

You carry concern in your heart because you love deeply. Because protecting your children matters to you. Because you want them safe, covered, and guided even when you cannot be everywhere at once.

It is exhausting to hold responsibility you cannot fully control.

God sees your worry. He understands the weight you carry. He is not asking you to stop caring. He is inviting you to release what you cannot hold alone.

Your children are not outside of God s care.

They are not unseen.

They are not uncovered.

You can rest knowing that what you cannot reach, God can. What you cannot fix, God can guide. What you cannot protect at every moment, God can surround.

SCRIPTURE

All your children will be taught by the Lord, and great will be their peace. Isaiah 54:13

This is a promise that God is involved in the lives of your children even when you are not present.

◊◊◊

Train up a child in the way he should go, and when he is old, he will not depart from it. Proverbs 22:6

Your influence matters. Your prayers matter. Seeds you planted continue to grow.

DECLARATION

I release my children into God s care.

I trust that they are covered even when I worry.

I choose peace over fear.

I am not carrying this alone.

PRAYER

God, You see the weight I carry as a mother.

You know the thoughts that keep me up, the prayers I whisper, and the fears I do not always say out loud.

I place my children into Your hands, trusting that You love them even more than I do.

Cover them when I cannot see them. Protect them when I cannot reach them. Guide them when they have to make decisions on their own.

Guard their minds, their hearts, and their steps.

Surround them with the right people, the right influences, and the right direction.

When fear tries to rise within me, remind me that You are already where they are.

Give me peace in the places where I feel powerless.

Help me to trust You more than I trust my worry.

I release them into Your care, knowing they are never outside of Your reach.

In Jesus' name,

Amen.

A Prayer of Protection

Psalm 91

God, I choose to dwell in You.

I rest in Your shelter and trust in Your protection.

Cover me under Your wings.

Guard my heart, my mind, and my home.

Protect me from harm seen and unseen.

When fear rises, remind me that You are near.

When danger feels close, remind me that You are greater.

I declare that You are my refuge and my fortress.

My God, in whom I trust.

I receive Your peace.

I walk in Your covering.

I rest in Your care.

In Jesus' name,

Amen.

When The Storm Feels Lonely

There are seasons when the storm feels heavier because it is quiet.

No crowd. No explanations. No one standing beside you saying, I see it too.

If you are here, still showing up, still pouring, still trying to uplift others, while quietly walking through one of your heaviest seasons, this word is for you.

Sometimes the storm is not meant to be shared.

Not because you are meant to suffer, but because you are being strengthened in ways that only solitude can form.

There are moments when God allows the noise to fall away so you can hear Him clearly.

Moments when support feels limited so your roots can grow deeper.

Moments when you learn that your strength is not dependent on who is standing with you, but on who is holding you.

Going through something alone does not mean you are abandoned.

It means this season is shaping your discernment, your compassion, and your authority.

Some storms refine you quietly so you can later stand before others and say,

I know this road. And you are not alone.

If this season feels heavier than the last, it is because you are being entrusted with more.

You are still held.

You are still covered.

You are still anchored.

Still Anchored When Life Moves Forward

Life does not always pause while you are healing.

The world keeps moving. Responsibilities remain. People still need you.

And somehow, you are expected to carry what you feel while continuing to show up.

There may be days when you wonder how you are still standing.

Days when you move forward, not because it is easy, but because it is necessary.

And even in that, there is strength.

Being anchored does not mean you are untouched by life.

It means you are not undone by it.

It means that even when everything around you shifts, something within you remains steady.

You are learning how to carry both healing and responsibility at the same time.

You are learning how to breathe again while still moving forward.

And that is not weakness.

That is growth.

That is resilience.

That is becoming.

You do not arrive at this place because everything is resolved.

You arrive here because you chose not to quit.

Still anchored does not mean you feel settled every day.

It means you know where to return when you don't.

This season is quieter.

Not easier, just quieter.

You may still carry unanswered questions.

You may still feel moments of fatigue or doubt.

But now, you recognize the difference between falling apart and simply needing rest.

You are not rebuilding yourself from scratch.

You are learning how to live with greater awareness, honesty, and grace.

What Staying Anchored Looks Like Now

It looks like choosing peace without explaining it.

It looks like honoring your limits.

It looks like trusting your pace.

You no longer need to prove your strength by pushing through everything.

Strength now shows up as discernment.

As boundaries.

As knowing when to pause.

Still anchored means you are no longer defined by what you endured,

but by how intentionally you move forward.

Staying anchored does not mean you have all the answers.

It does not mean you no longer feel pain, or that every day is easy.

It means you have learned where to return when life feels uncertain.

It looks like trusting God in moments where you once would have spiraled.

It looks like setting boundaries, protecting your heart, and honoring your growth.

It looks like giving yourself grace on the days that feel heavier.

It looks like continuing, even when you have to move slower than before.

It looks like quiet strength.

It looks like steady faith.

It looks like not giving up on yourself.

And even now, you are doing better than you think.

You are still here.

You are still growing.

You are still anchored.

Final Blessing and Covering

As you close this book, may peace go with you.

Not the kind of peace that ignores pain, but the kind that steadies you in the middle of it.

May you remember that every season you have walked through mattered.

The tears you cried mattered.

The strength it took to keep going mattered.

And the woman you are becoming matters.

May God cover you when life feels uncertain.

May He guard your heart, your mind, and your path.

May He bring rest where you have been weary and hope where you have been waiting.

When fear tries to rise, may peace meet you.

When grief returns, may comfort surround you.

When strength feels distant, may grace hold you.

Wherever life takes you from here, may you walk forward covered, protected, and at peace.

And may you always remember that no matter the season, you are anchored.

You do not have to explain this season.

You do not have to explain why you are tired.

You do not have to prove your strength.

You only have to remain.

And even here, especially here, you are anchored.

Daily Reflections & Prayers

A Week of Grounding, Strength, and Peace

An Invitation to Begin Again, Every Day

These daily reflections and prayers are not meant to be rushed, completed, or perfected. They are here to meet you where you are whether you arrive steady or scattered, hopeful or weary.

Some days, you may read a single paragraph and feel anchored.
Other days, you may only whisper the prayer at the bottom of the page.
Both are enough.

This section is designed to be a gentle rhythm, not a rigid routine. You are not behind if you miss a day. You are not failing if your heart feels heavy. You are not weak if you need to return to the same reflection more than once.

Each day offers space to:

- pause and reflect,
- realign your thoughts with truth,
- pray honestly,
- and declare what you are choosing to stand on.

You may move through these days in order, return to the one that speaks most clearly to your season, or rest on a single page longer than planned. There is no right way to engage—only an invitation to remain anchored.

Let these pages remind you that:

- healing does not require urgency,
- growth does not demand perfection,
- and God meets you faithfully in the ordinary moments of your day.

As you begin, take a breath.
You are not starting from scratch.
You are starting from strength.

You are anchored and you are allowed to begin again.

MINDSET MONDAY

Aligning Your Thoughts with Truth

REFLECTION

How you think shapes how you move through the day. Before the conversations begin and the responsibilities pile up, your thoughts are already setting the tone.

Some mornings, your mind wakes up heavy. Old worries resurface. Fear speaks louder than faith. Doubt reminds you of what feels unfinished, uncertain, or overwhelming. Without realizing it, you may find yourself carrying yesterday's weight into today.

This is your reminder that you do not have to believe every thought that enters your mind.

Mindset Monday is not about forcing positivity or pretending everything is okay. It is about gently bringing your thoughts back to what is true. Choosing alignment over anxiety. Truth over fear. Peace over pressure.

You do not need to have everything figured out today. You only need to begin grounded in truth.

SCRIPTURE

Do not conform to the pattern of this world, but be transformed by the renewing of your mind." Romans 12:2

PRAYER

God, today I bring You my thoughts, the anxious ones, the heavy ones, the ones shaped by fear and exhaustion. I ask You to renew my mind where it has grown tired and overwhelmed.

Help me recognize thoughts that are not serving my peace and gently release them. Replace confusion with clarity. Replace fear with trust. Replace pressure with calm assurance.

Anchor my thoughts in what is true, not what feels loud or urgent. As I move through this day, guide my thinking, steady my emotions, and remind me that I am not walking alone.

Amen.

DECLARATION

I choose truth over fear.

I release anxious and unhelpful thoughts.

My mind is grounded.

My thoughts are aligned.

I am anchored.

TESTIMONY TUESDAY

Remembering What You ve Survived

REFLECTION

It is easy to focus on what is still ahead and forget how far you have already come. Pain has a way of overshadowing progress, and struggle can make survival feel ordinary.

But your story matters.

Testimony is not only about public victories or dramatic breakthroughs. It is about the quiet strength it took to endure. The resilience it required to keep going when life felt heavy. The grace that carried you through moments you never thought you would survive.

Today is an invitation to remember — not with pain, but with perspective. You are still here. And that is not by accident.

SCRIPTURE

They overcame by the blood of the Lamb and by the word of their testimony." Revelation 12:11

PRAYER

God, thank You for carrying me through moments I did not think I would survive. Thank You for the strength You gave me when mine felt depleted.

Help me remember my story with honesty and grace. Heal the places where pain still lingers and remind me that my survival is evidence of Your faithfulness.

When discouragement tries to speak louder than truth, anchor me in what You have already brought me through. Let my testimony strengthen my faith today.

Amen.

DECLARATION

I honor what I have survived.

I acknowledge the strength it took to keep going.

My story matters.

My endurance is real.

I am anchored

WORTHY WEDNESDAY

Remembering What Is Already Yours

REFLECTION

You are worthy of love, peace, joy, and happiness. Not because you earned it. Not because you got everything right. But because God promised it to you.

Life may have tried to convince you otherwise. Pain can distort truth. Disappointment can make you forget what was spoken over you long before the storm arrived.

Today is a reminder.

You do not have to fight for what God freely gives. You do not have to shrink to be accepted. You do not have to settle for less than what He promised.

Let this be the day you stop questioning your worth and start resting in it.

SCRIPTURE

For the Lord takes delight in His people." Psalm 149:4

PRAYER

God, today I need to be reminded of what is true. There have been moments when I questioned my worth and doubted whether love, peace, and joy were meant for me.

Heal the places where I learned to believe I had to earn what You freely give. Quiet every lie that told me I was undeserving or forgotten. Help me receive Your promises without guilt or fear.

Anchor my heart in the truth of who I am in You. Teach me to rest in what You have already declared over my life.

Amen.

DECLARATION

I am worthy of love, peace, joy, and happiness.

I receive what God has promised me.

I release doubt and comparison.

I am anchored in truth.

THANKFUL THURSDAY

Finding Gratitude Even Here

REFLECTION

Gratitude does not deny pain. It simply creates space for perspective. You can be thankful and still hurting. You can acknowledge blessings while honoring what feels heavy.

Today is not about forcing joy. It is about noticing what remains steady, even in the middle of uncertainty. Sometimes gratitude is quiet. Sometimes it is simply acknowledging that you made it through another day.

And that is enough.

SCRIPTURE

Give thanks in all circumstances."
I Thessalonians 5:18

PRAYER

God, open my eyes to see what I have overlooked. Even in difficult moments, help me recognize the grace You continue to give.

Teach me to hold gratitude gently, without pressure or guilt. Thank You for what You have carried me through and for what You are still doing, even when I cannot see it clearly.

Anchor my heart in appreciation, not perfection.

Amen.

DECLARATION

I choose gratitude today.

I acknowledge the good without denying the hard.

Even here, I am thankful.

I remain anchored.

FAITHFUL FRIDAY

Choosing Trust Again

REFLECTION

Some seasons stretch your faith quietly. You are still praying, still believing, but tired of waiting. Trust feels heavier when answers take longer than expected.

Faithful Friday is not about loud declarations. It is about choosing trust again — gently, honestly, and without pretending.

You do not need perfect faith. You only need a willing heart.

SCRIPTURE

Trust in the Lord with all your heart." Proverbs 3:5

PRAYER

God, today I bring You my tired faith. I admit the moments when trusting You has felt difficult or uncertain.

Strengthen what feels weak. Restore what has grown weary. Help me trust You beyond what I see or understand. Anchor my heart when answers feel delayed.

I place my confidence in You again today, knowing You are faithful even when the journey feels long.

Amen.

DECLARATION

I choose trust over fear.

I release the need to control outcomes.

My faith is held.

My heart is anchored.

SUCCESSFUL SATURDAY

Redefining What Success Really Looks Like

REFLECTION

Success does not always look like finished goals or visible achievements. Sometimes success looks like surviving a week that demanded more than you felt able to give.

If you showed up when you wanted to hide, that matters. If you kept going while carrying silent weight, that matters. If you are still standing, that matters.

Endurance is not invisible to God. Every quiet victory counts.

SCRIPTURE

Come to Me, all who are weary and burdened, and I will give you rest." Matthew 11:28–30

PRAYER

God, thank You for seeing what others may not notice. The effort, the perseverance, the strength it took to keep going this week.

Help me release unrealistic expectations and comparisons. Teach me to honor progress, not perfection.

Thank You for carrying me through moments I didn t think I could face.

Anchor my heart in the truth that endurance matters and that surviving is success in Your eyes.

Amen.

DECLARATION

I honor the strength it took to make it here.

My perseverance is seen.

I am not behind.

I am successful.

I am anchored.

SELF-CARE SUNDAY

Returning to Yourself

REFLECTION

Self-care is not selfish. It is stewardship. You were never meant to pour endlessly without being replenished.

Today is about gentleness. Listening to your needs. Honoring your limits. Allowing rest to restore what has been poured out.

You deserve care too.

SCRIPTURE

Come to Me, all who are weary." Mathew11:28-30

PRAYER

God, help me care for myself the way You desire. Teach me to rest without guilt and set boundaries without apology.

Restore my spirit, renew my strength, and remind me that tending to my heart matters. Anchor me in gentleness as I prepare for the days ahead.

Thank You for meeting me in rest and restoring what has been worn down.

Amen.

DECLARATION

I honor my needs with compassion.

I choose rest and renewal.

I am cared for.

I am restored.

I am anchored.

A NOTE FROM ME TO YOU

Rooted. Rising. Anchored.

If you're here, it means you made it through the pages and I don't take that lightly.

I don't know exactly what you were carrying when you first opened this book.
But I know what it feels like to pick something up while your heart is heavy, your mind is tired, and your strength feels thinner than you'd like to admit.

My prayer is that somewhere along the way, maybe not all at once, maybe not even noticeably but things began to feel a little lighter.
That a sentence slowed your breathing.
That a prayer put words to what you couldn't say.
That a reminder met you right where you were.

If you're not there" yet, that's okay too.
Healing doesn't rush, and neither does God.

I want you to know that you are not alone not in what you've faced, not in what you're still carrying, and not in what comes next. I am praying for you. I am standing with you in faith, believing that what once felt overwhelming will not have the final word.

You don't have to have everything figured out.
You don't have to be stronger than you are today.

You don't have to rush into the next chapter of your life.
You are allowed to move forward gently.
And here is what I know to be true:
When you are anchored in God, you are also being rooted.
Rooted in truth. Rooted in faith. Rooted deeper than the storm ever reached.
And when you are rooted, growth is inevitable.

Rising does not mean the storm never happened.
It means it didn't uproot you.

So if all you can do right now is stand still you are still growing.
If you are healing quietly, you are still rising.
If you feel unseen but sustained, you are still anchored.

If this book helped you pause, breathe, reflect, or reconnect, even for a moment, then it has done what it was meant to do.

Remain anchored.
Stay rooted.
And when the time is right.

RISE.

With love and prayer,
Dr. Tamika Andrea

A Prayer Spoken Over You

Father God in Heaven,

I come to You as humble as I know how, on behalf of Your daughter, the one reading these words right now.

Lord, You made her.
You formed her with intention.
You know her name, her story, her tears, and the prayers she never spoke out loud.

Before anyone ever misunderstood her, You knew her.
Before anything tried to break her, You covered her.

God, I thank You for always shielding her.
For always protecting her.
For standing between her and every weapon that formed against her and not allowing a single one to prosper.

Lord, thank You for not letting the pain she endured stop her from reaching this moment right here.
Thank You for the nights she survived, the tears she cried in private, and the strength You gave her when she didn't know how she would make it through.

Thank You for sustaining her when she felt weak.
For carrying her when she couldn't carry herself.
For guarding her heart even when she felt exposed.

Father, I thank You for her life.
For her purpose.
For what lies ahead of her.

Thank You that what tried to destroy her did not win.
What tried to silence her did not prevail.
What tried to delay her could not cancel what You have already ordained.

God, I ask You now to surround her with Your peace, not the kind the world offers, but the kind that anchors her soul.
Quiet her mind.
Strengthen her heart.
Restore what has been worn down by time, loss, and disappointment.

Cover her family.
Cover her home.
Cover her future.

Let her know that she is not behind, not forgotten, and not overlooked.

Remind her that You are still working on her behalf, no matter what it looks like.

Father, root her deeply in You.
Anchor her firmly in truth.
And in Your perfect timing, allow her to rise healed, whole, and confident in who You created her to be.

We declare that she is protected.
She is chosen.
She is loved.
And she is highly Favored by You.

And it is in the mighty, matchless name of Jesus that I pray,

Amen.

ABOUT THE AUTHOR

Before anything else, Tamika Andrea is a woman who understands what it feels like to carry strength and still feel tired. She knows the weight of responsibility, the quiet prayers whispered in the dark, and the courage it takes to keep going when life feels heavy. This book was written from that place, not as someone who has it all figured out, but as someone who has learned how to stay anchored through the storm.

Pastor Dr. Tamika Andrea is a faith-centered leader, author, and advocate whose work is rooted in strength, restoration, and community empowerment.

Her voice is shaped not only by calling, but by the storms she has personally weathered. Seasons of loss, uncertainty, responsibility, and quiet endurance have deepened her compassion and strengthened her to walk alongside others with honesty and grace.

As a pastor, mentor, and mother, she understands what it means to show up for others while carrying weight that is rarely seen. Her ministry and writing are grounded in lived experience, faith, and the belief that healing and peace are possible even in the middle of life s hardest seasons.

Dr. Tamika Andrea is the Pastor of W.O.R. International Ministries and the founder of Women Uplifting Women, a movement created to destroy the spirit of envy, jealousy, and competition among women while building a platform of true unity, genuine love, and support. Through this work, she is committed to standing in the gap for women during their most challenging moments.

Anchored was written as a reflection of her own journey and as a companion for women who need a place to breathe, be honest, and return to peace. It is offered with the understanding that storms do not disqualify you. They shape you.

STAY CONNECTED

If this book met you in a meaningful way and you desire continued encouragement or prayer, you are welcome to connect with Women Uplifting Women.

Women Uplifting Women exists to create a safe space for women to grow, heal, and support one another through every season of life.

Visit: WUWNetwork.com

www.ingramcontent.com/pod-product-compliance
Lightning Source LLC
LaVergne TN
LVHW010936110826
845149LV00013B/2628
9781957904214